B1

LEARNING TO CONNECT WORDS & RELATIONSHIPS

Think Analogies® Series

📖 A1 📖 B1

Written by

Cheryl Block

© 2001
THE CRITICAL THINKING CO.™
www.CriticalThinking.com
Phone: 800-458-4849 • Fax: 831-393-3277
P.O. Box 1610 • Seaside • CA 93955-1610
ISBN 978-0-89455-792-7

This book is dedicated to my two wonderful children, Lisa and Brian, both of whom are aspiring teachers.

You are my joy and inspiration.

Table of Contents

Introduction

Students who learn strategies to make and complete analogies benefit in many ways. Students sharpen their reasoning skills as they analyze the subtleties of language and relationship presented in analogies. Analogies are useful tools for developing students' grasp of concepts and ideas in content areas. As students learn to understand simple word analogies, they move towards understanding more complex analogous relationships presented in literature, science, and history. Analogies are also a key component of many assessment and ability tests.

Analogies make comparisons between seemingly unrelated items. Comparing an unfamiliar item to an item that is more familiar increases understanding. The similarity between the items is based on the relationship being compared, not the items themselves. For instance, a suction cup is a good analogy for the tube feet on a starfish. Initially it is easier for students to find similarities between related items. Gradually, however, you want to move students towards looking for similarities between unrelated items.

Students analyze relationships between the items being compared. In the example below, the student must look at parts of the human body and determine how these parts relate to one another.

	a. acid	:	stomach
Example: mouth is to eat AS	**b.** stomach	:	liver
	c. teeth	:	chew
	d. tongue	:	mouth

Students must first recognize the relationship of "mouth" to "eat." A mouth is a part of the body that is used *to* eat. Next they look at the relationships in the choices given. In choice a, acid is a *product of* the stomach. This is not the same kind of relationship. (A similar relationship would be that the stomach is used to digest.) In choice b, the stomach and the liver are both kinds *of* organs. In choice d, the tongue is part *of* the mouth. Only choice c has the same kind of relationship: teeth are used *to* chew.

The key to analogies is the relationship between the word pairs. Students must learn to find similarities between the two pairs. Initially, this is easier to do with items that are related. Gradually, however, students should look for similarities between items that seem to be unrelated.

	a. leaf is to branch
	b. door is to house
Example: bark is to tree AS	**c.** skin is to human
	d. acorn is to oak

Many students would select **a.** Bark is part of a tree, and a leaf is part of a branch. However, a tree is a general category of plant; a branch is part of a tree. The relationship between a leaf and a branch is different from the relationship between bark and a tree. The other relationship that is similar to this is choice **c.** Bark is the outer surface of a tree that protects it. Our skin is also an outer surface that protects us. What makes these items analogous is the relationship they share.

Activities in this book develop sequentially, with one skill building upon another. Students classify words with a common attribute and find exceptions. They then form pairs of related items. Next they identify types of analogous relationships. They practice classifying different kinds of analogies and selecting words and word pairs to complete them. Finally, they create analogies.

Finding Common Attributes

What does each group of things have in common?

1. bottle, jar, box, bin _____

2. mirror, bottle, window, spectacles _____

3. web, fishnet, lace, basket _____

4. plate, tire, coin, CD _____

5. sandpaper, burlap, bark, concrete _____

6. snow, cloud, foam, baby powder _____

7. fog, steam, smoke, cloud _____

8. cork, feather, leaf, apple _____

9. perfume, flower, vanilla, lavender _____

10. tape, staple, pin, rubber band _____

11. fur, feather, skin, scales _____

12. artichoke, cactus, rose, porcupine _____

13. river, tree, college, science _____

14. diatom, cell, bacteria, plankton _____

15. idiom, metaphor, simile, hyperbole _____

Finding the Exception

Circle the word in each group that doesn't belong. Explain why.

1. tongs, sieve, (wrench,) spatula, spoon <u>All cooking tools except the wrench.</u>

2. silk, cotton, leather, vinyl, wool _____

3. seam, hem, margin, sleeve, lining _____

4. alligator, snake, lizard, shark, turtle _____

5. gallon, pint, pound, quart, liter _____

6. ivy, wisteria, grape, squash, potato _____

7. heron, robin, owl, ostrich, pelican _____

8. rhombus, square, sphere, octagon, circle _____

9. weasel, cougar, deer, rat, bear _____

10. pink, magenta, crimson, ochre, scarlet _____

11. verb, noun, prefix, adverb, pronoun _____

12. arm, hand, heart, leg, foot _____

13. book, journal, letter, photo, recipe _____

14. coupe, sedan, catamaran, hardtop, compact _____

15. lemon, orange, pear, lime, grapefruit _____

Seeing Relationships

Analogies are based on relationships between word pairs. There is often more than one way to build a relationship between pairs of words. Using the following group of words, look at the different ways these words can be related.

fish, fin, fly, worm, swim, wing, bird

1. Look at the first example below. In the first pair of words, **swim** is the action that a fish does. What is the action that a bird does?

fish/swim   bird/_____

In each pair, the first item is followed by its action.

2. Look at the next example. In this example, a fin is part of a fish. What is a wing part of?

fin/fish   wing/_____

In each pair, the first item is part of the second item.

3. Complete the last example. How is *fin* related to *swim*? What word above relates to *wing* in the same way?

fin/swim   wing/_____

In the example above, the first item is something used to do the second item.

Remember that words can have more than one meaning. What is the relationship below if *fly* is a noun? Fill in the missing word and explain the relationship.

fish/fly   bird/_____

Explain: _____

_____

Making Word Pairs

DIRECTIONS: What are some possible word pairs you could make using the words in each group? T he words should be related in some way.

oak, tree, leaf, deer

Example: oak/tree: an oak is a kind of tree; leaf/tree: a leaf is a part of a tree (or an oak); deer/leaf: a deer eats a leaf

1. arm, ball, throw, boy

    _____

    _____

2. wall, fence, board, wood

    _____

    _____

3. fish, school, boy, swim

    _____

    _____

4. flag, wave, sea, ship

    _____

    _____

5. cover, lid, quilt, blanket

    _____

    _____

Classifying Word Pairs

How would you classify these two pairs of words?

1. pore/skin   2. stoma/leaf

First decide how each pair of words is related.

In each pair, the first item is *a part of* the second item.

Now describe the relationship.

A pore is an opening in the human skin through which the body releases moisture or sweat. A stoma is an opening in the surface of a leaf through which the plant releases water and oxygen.

Classify the following word pairs. Describe how each pair of words is related.

1. lion/pride, horse/herd

   _____
   _____
   _____

2. beetle/insect, crab/crustacean

   _____
   _____
   _____

3. wool/sheep, leather/cattle

   _____
   _____
   _____

What Is an Analogy?

An analogy is a comparison between two word pairs. The key to understanding analogies is to focus on the relationship between the word pairs. For example:

guppy is to fish AS hawk is to bird

In each pair of the analogy, the first animal is a specific kind of the second animal. A guppy is a kind of fish, and a hawk is a kind of bird.

The relationship between the two pairs should be clear even if the words seem unrelated. Look at the next example.

feather is to bird AS fiberglass is to house

Feathers insulate a bird; fiberglass insulates a house. Both help to provide warmth.

There should be a reason for the relationship. Don't make up a relationship that isn't really necessary. For example:

rope is to tow AS hair is to pull

You use a rope to tow something, like an animal or a boat. When you tow something, you pull it. You can pull hair, but that isn't something that needs to be done to hair. You don't usually use hair to tow something. What is another item that is used for pulling?

rope is to tow AS leash is to lead

A leash is used to lead or pull an animal.

Clues to Reading Analogies

1. Analogies can be written in words or in symbols. The dots replace the words.

hawk is to bird AS guppy is to fish

hawk : bird :: guppy : fish

Both of these analogies read: A hawk *is related to* a bird *in the same way as* a guppy *is related to* a fish.

2. The order of the words may vary. The most common arrangement of words in an analogy is word 1 is related to word 2 as word 3 is related to word 4.

hawk is to bird AS guppy is to fish

1 is to 2 AS 3 is to 4

The analogy reads: A hawk is a kind of bird as a guppy is a kind of fish.

However, the same analogy can also be arranged in a 1 is to 3 as 2 is to 4 order.

hawk is to guppy AS bird is to fish

The analogy still reads: A hawk is a kind of bird, and a guppy is a kind of fish.

3. When reading an analogy, look at the parts of speech used in each word pair. The types of words used give you a clue as to the type of relationship shown. In an analogy with a *kind of* relationship, the words are all nouns.

pear is to fruit AS squash is to vegetable

In an object/action analogy, the first word is a noun, the object, and the second word is a verb, the action.

bird is to chirp AS dog is to bark

Reading Analogies

Look at the arrangement of words in each analogy below. Write what the analogy says.

Example: scissors is to cut AS pen is to write

Scissors is an object used to cut just as a pen is an object used to write.

1.   bristle is to brush AS tooth is to comb

   _____

   _____

2.   veterinarian is to animals AS physician is to people

   _____

   _____

3.   rabbit is to wolf AS herbivore is to carnivore

   _____

   _____

4.   narrow is to wide AS crevice is to crevasse

   _____

   _____

5.   inflate is to expand AS deflate is to shrink

   _____

   _____

Classifying Analogies

Analogies are classified by the type of relationship shown between the word pairs. What relationship is shown in the analogy below?

teacher *is to* faculty AS principal *is to* administration

A teacher is *part of* a faculty, and a principal is *part of* the administration. Both are parts of groups in the field of education. This analogy would be classified as a *part-whole* relationship.

How would you classify the next analogy? Look carefully at the relationship between each pair of words.

Dalmatian : leopard : : zebra : tiger

Dalmatian and leopard are both *kinds of* animals. A Dalmatian and a leopard also have spotted skin. A zebra and a tiger are both *kinds of* animals. A zebra and a tiger also have striped skin. You would classify this relationship as a *kind of* relationship. In this case, the first pair is *kinds of animals with spots,* and the second pair is *kinds of animals with stripes.* If you replaced the word *tiger* with the word *lion*, would the analogy work as well?

Classify the next two analogies according to the following categories: *part of, kind of, synonym,* or *antonym.* Explain the relationship.

uncle *is to* aunt AS nephew *is to* niece

1. _____

_____

pedestal *is to* statue AS tripod *is to* camera

2. _____

_____

Classification Analogies

Kind of

1. In each pair, the first item is a specific kind of the second item. Both words in each pair are nouns.

worm is to parasite AS human is to host

A worm is a kind of parasite, and a human is a kind of host.

2. The first two items are the same kind of thing, and the second two items are the same kind of thing. Both words in each pair are nouns.

lizard is to snake AS camel is to moose

A lizard and a snake are *both reptiles*. A camel and a moose are *both mammals*.

Part-Whole

1. In each pair, the first item is a part of a whole thing, the second item. Both words in each pair are nouns.

cockpit is to plane AS bridge is to ship

A cockpit is the part of the plane where the pilot flies. The bridge is the part of the ship where the captain guides the ship and directs the crew.

2. In each pair, the first item belongs to a group of things, the second item. Both words in each pair are nouns.

athlete is to team AS spectator is to audience

An athlete can be part of a group of players on a team. A spectator is part of a group of spectators in an audience.

Product of

1. The first item is a product of the second item which is a source. Both words in each pair are nouns.

glass *is to* **sand** AS **steel** *is to* **iron**

Glass is a product of sand, and steel is a product of iron.

2. The first item is a product of a process, the second item. Both words in each pair are nouns.

nitrogen *is to* **decomposition** AS **oxygen** *is to* **photosynthesis**

Nitrogen is produced in the decomposition process of plants and animals. Oxygen is produced in the process of photosynthesis in plants.

Classification Analogies—Select

DIRECTIONS: Classify the following analogies as

a) part of

b) kind of

c) product of

1. book is to library AS food is to market   _____

2. skirt is to blouse AS pants is to jacket   _____

3. blood is to vein AS marrow is to bone   _____

4. pouch is to kangaroo AS hump is to camel   _____

5. butter is to churning AS yogurt is to curdling   _____

6. den is to lair AS aerie is to nest   _____

7. down is to goose AS silk is to worm   _____

8. tea is to leaf AS coffee is to bean   _____

9. water is to lake AS sand is to desert   _____

10. heat is to combustion AS rust is to oxidation   _____

11. oyster is to bivalve AS snail is to univalve   _____

12. blowhole is to whale AS gill is to fish   _____

13. scallion is to onion AS zucchini is to squash   _____

14. ladybug is to beetle AS monarch is to butterfly   _____

15. butter is to cream AS cake is to batter   _____

Comparative Analogies

Synonyms

In each pair, the first word means the same as the second word.

satchel *is to* bag AS crate *is to* box

Satchel is another word, or synonym, for *bag*. The words *crate* and *box* are synonyms. All four items are kinds of containers.

Antonyms

In each pair, the first word means the opposite of the second word.

convex *is to* concave AS outward *is to* inward

Convex means curved outward; *concave* means curved inward.

Sequences

1. In each pair of items, there is a progression in time, order, or rank from the first item to the second. Usually, both words in each pair are nouns. The following analogy is arranged in order of time.

evening *is to* night AS Sunday *is to* Monday

Evening comes before night, and Sunday comes before Monday. In the next example, each pair is arranged in order of size.

guppy *is to* trout AS cod *is to* shark

A guppy is smaller than a trout, and a tuna is smaller than a shark. Also, all four words are arranged in order from smallest to largest.

2. Each pair of items shows steps in a process. All words are verbs.

cook *is to* eat AS write *is to* mail

You cook the food before you eat it; you write the letter before you mail it.

Comparative Analogies—Select

DIRECTIONS: Classify the following analogies as

    a) antonyms   b) synonyms   c) sequence

1. core is to crust AS inner is to outer   _____

2. inspect is to examine AS study is to explore   _____

3. egg is to larva AS pupa is to butterfly   _____

4. bold is to timid AS fearless is to afraid   _____

5. march is to tramp AS tread is to walk   _____

6. rich is to poor AS wealthy is to needy   _____

7. rare is to medium AS well-done is to burnt   _____

8. parasite is to host AS predator is to prey   _____

9. glory is to fame AS honor is to renown   _____

10. dirty is to clean AS filthy is to immaculate   _____

11. roam is to wander AS stray is to ramble   _____

12. inch is to foot AS centimeter is to meter   _____

13. active is to lively AS idle is to listless   _____

14. mix is to separate AS combine is to divide   _____

15. sensible is to foolish AS knowledgeable is to ignorant   _____

Classifying Analogies

DIRECTIONS: Read the analogy and decide how each word pair is related. Choose the correct type of analogy from the box below, and write the letter on the line to the right. State the relationship shown in the analogy.

a. part of	b. sequence	c. product of	d. antonym

1. tree : grove :: flower : bouquet ___a___
   A tree is part of a grove of trees; a flower is part of a bouquet of flowers.

2. music : piano :: photo : camera ___

3. skeleton : body :: framework : house ___

4. small : medium :: petite : average ___

5. fresh : stale :: crisp : wilted ___

6. cola : nut :: chocolate : bean ___

7. tributary : river :: capillary : artery ___

Classifying Analogies

DIRECTIONS: Read the analogy and decide how each word pair is related. Choose the correct type of analogy from the box below, and write the letter on the line to the right. State the relationship shown in the analogy.

a. part of	b. kind of	c. antonym	d. synonym

1. plant : producer :: rabbit : consumer   _____

2. gather : scatter :: combine : separate   _____

3. ice : solid :: water : liquid   _____

4. lawyer : attorney :: doctor : physician   _____

5. scales : reptile :: hair : mammal   _____

6. humid : damp :: arid : dry   _____

7. actor : cast :: sailor : crew   _____

8. simple : easy :: complex : hard   _____

9. freezing : physical :: burning : chemical   _____

10. scene : play :: stanza : poem   _____

11. authentic : genuine :: counterfeit : fake   _____

12. drizzle : downpour :: breeze : gale   _____

13. sketch : drawing :: blueprint : diagram   _____

14. wheel : bicycle :: tire : automobile   _____

Classifying Analogies

DIRECTIONS: Read the analogy and decide how each word pair is related. Then choose the correct type of analogy from the box below, and write the letter on the line.

a. synonym	b. kind of	c. sequence	d. product of

1. infant : toddler :: teen : adult   _____

2. steam : geyser :: lava : volcano   _____

3. glue : adhesive :: oil : lubricant   _____

4. book : author :: song : composer   _____

5. penny : nickel :: dime : quarter   _____

6. quarrel : dispute :: truce : treaty   _____

7. limber : flexible :: stiff : rigid   _____

8. windbreaker : jacket :: windsurfer : athlete   _____

9. summer : fall :: winter : spring   _____

10. spore : fern :: seed : flower   _____

11. citadel : fortress :: tower : turret   _____

12. dew : liquid :: steam : gas   _____

13. abandon : leave :: remain : stay   _____

14. saliva : mouth :: bile : liver   _____

Descriptive Analogies

Characteristic of

1. The first word is an adjective that describes a quality of the second word.

   ### rough *is to* sandpaper AS smooth *is to* silk

   Sandpaper has a rough texture, and silk has a smooth texture.

2. The first word is a noun that describes a characteristic of the second word.

   ### flexibility *is to* muscle AS rigidity *is to* bone

Association

1. The first item is associated with the second in an implied relationship.

   ### island *is to* ocean AS oasis *is to* desert

   An island is not part of the ocean but is usually found in the ocean. An oasis is not part of the desert but is usually found in the desert.

   ### desert *is to* Southwest AS plains *is to* Midwest

   Desert is usually associated with the southwestern United States. Plains are usually associated with the midwestern United States.

Object-Action

1. The first word is a noun that names an object. The second word is a verb that describes an action of the first.

   ### horse *is to* trot AS snake *is to* slither

   A horse trots and a snake slithers.

Something Used to

1. In each pair, the first item names an object. The second item is a verb that describes how the first item is used.

bicycle *is to* ride AS car *is to* drive

A bicycle is a vehicle you ride, and a car is a vehicle you drive. This analogy is different from the object-action analogy because a bicycle does not ride itself. Someone has to ride a bicycle.

2. In each pair, the first item names an object. The second item is a noun that describes something with which the object is used.

wrench *is to* pipes AS saw *is to* wood

A wrench is used to tighten or loosen pipes; a saw is used to cut wood.

Someone Who

1. In each pair, the first item names a person, and the second item is a verb that describes what the person does.

chauffeur *is to* drive AS pilot *is to* fly

A chauffeur drives a car; a pilot flies a plane.

2. In each pair, the first word names a person, and the second word tells what that person uses in his/her job, or who that person works with.

chauffeur *is to* limousine AS pilot *is to* plane

A chauffeur drives a limousine; a pilot flies a plane.

3. In each pair, the first word names a person, and the second word names a person with whom the first person works.

doctor *is to* patient AS lawyer *is to* client

A doctor takes care of a patient; a lawyer takes care of a client.

Descriptive Analogies—Select

DIRECTIONS: Classify the following analogies as

a) used to   b) object–action   c) characteristic

1. cold is to glacier AS heat is to volcano   _____

2. sugar is to dissolve AS flour is to mix   _____

3. period is to stop AS comma is to pause   _____

4. thin is to thread AS thick is to rope   _____

5. horse is to gallop AS gazelle is to leap   _____

6. volcano is to erupt AS fault is to split   _____

7. siphon is to drain AS funnel is to pour   _____

8. flower is to bloom AS seed is to sprout   _____

9. period is to sentence AS stoplight is to traffic   _____

10. thick is to mud AS thin is to water   _____

11. velocity is to speed AS frequency is to sound   _____

12. gale is to blow AS cloud is to drift   _____

13. motion is to river AS stillness is to pond   _____

14. diesel is to truck AS propellant is to rocket   _____

15. sweet is to tart AS orange is to lemon   _____

Descriptive Analogies—Select

DIRECTIONS: Classify the following analogies as

a) someone who   b) used to   c) association

1.   beach is to tropics AS iceberg is to Arctic   _____

2.   wave is to ocean AS dune is to desert   _____

3.   prefix is to begin AS suffix is to end   _____

4.   lawyer is to client AS teacher is to student   _____

5.   pharmacist is to dispense AS physician is to prescribe   _____

6.   ledger is to accounts AS calendar is to dates   _____

7.   compost is to organic AS plastic is to synthetic   _____

8.   jester is to comedy AS troubadour is to music   _____

9.   jewels is to wealth AS rags is to poverty   _____

10. immigrant is to settle AS migrant is to travel   _____

11. inch is to length AS square inch is to area   _____

12. radar is to distance AS sonar is to depth   _____

13. lecture is to audience AS conversation is to friend   _____

14. dictionary is to define AS encyclopedia is to explain   _____

15. chef is to cook AS waiter is to serve   _____

Classifying Analogies

DIRECTIONS: Read the analogy and decide how each word pair is related. Then choose the correct type of analogy from the box below, and write the letter on the line. Explain the relationship shown in the analogy.

a. used to	b. kind of	c. association	d. synonym

1. grass : producer :: rabbit : consumer   _____

    _____

2. president : democracy :: king : monarchy   _____

    _____

3. taffeta : fabric :: taffy : candy   _____

    _____

4. counterfeit : imitation :: genuine : real   _____

    _____

5. bridge : river :: overpass : freeway   _____

    _____

6. mild : gentle :: soft : tender   _____

    _____

7. oil : liquid :: nitrogen : gas   _____

    _____

Classifying Analogies

DIRECTIONS: Read the analogy and decide how each word pair is related. Then choose the correct type of analogy from the box below, and write the letter on the line. State the relationship shown in the analogy.

| a. object-action | b. sequence | c. characteristic | d. part of |

1. Stone Age : Bronze Age :: Dark Ages : Renaissance   _____

   _____

2. balloon : float :: bird : fly   _____

   _____

3. ribs : umbrella :: spokes : wheel   _____

   _____

4. white : milk :: clear : water   _____

   _____

5. tentacle : octopus :: tendril : plant   _____

   _____

6. lung : inflate :: diaphragm : contract   _____

   _____

7. cartilage : nose :: bone : jaw   _____

   _____

23

Classifying Analogies

DIRECTIONS: Read the analogy and decide how each word pair is related. Then choose the correct type of analogy from the box below, and write the letter on the line.

a. someone who	b. kind of	c. sequence	d. product of

1.   lawyer : argues :: judge : decides   _____

2.   pearl : oyster :: mother of pearl : abalone   _____

3.   kelp : algae :: mushroom : fungi   _____

4.   book : author :: song : composer   _____

5.   audition : rehearsal :: preview : performance   _____

6.   hygienist : dentist :: nurse : doctor   _____

7.   nectar : flower :: sap : tree   _____

8.   beetle : insect :: crab : crustacean   _____

9.   prepare : cook :: serve : dine   _____

10.   geologist : rock :: botanist : plant   _____

11.   cow : sheep :: moose : antelope   _____

12.   journalist : write :: editor : revise   _____

13.   none : one :: few : many   _____

14.   junior : senior :: middle school : high school   _____

Classifying Analogies

DIRECTIONS: Read the analogy and decide how each word pair is related. Then choose the correct type of analogy from the box below, and write the letter on the line.

a. antonym	b. part of	c. used to	d. product of

1. sawdust : wood :: chaff : wheat _____

2. aunt : family :: native : tribe _____

3. ebb : flow :: recede : proceed _____

4. amber : fossil :: ambergris : whale _____

5. cow : dairy :: hen : hatchery _____

6. eyedropper : medicine :: pipette : chemical _____

7. decibel : loudness :: fathom : depth _____

8. hasty : careful :: reckless : cautious _____

9. axis : wheel :: fulcrum : lever _____

10. brim : hat :: eave : roof _____

11. lighthouse : guide :: buoy : mark _____

12. residue : paint :: remnant : fabric _____

13. uncover : miss :: detect : overlook _____

14. mustard : seed :: ketchup : tomato _____

Classifying Analogies

DIRECTIONS: Read the analogy and decide how each word pair is related. Then choose the correct type of analogy from the box below, and write the letter on the line.

a. someone who	b. object-action	c. association	d. characteristic of

1. Venus : love :: Mars : war _____

2. consumer : buy :: merchant : sell _____

3. sticky : honey :: grainy : sugar _____

4. bee : pollinate :: seed : germinate _____

5. food : famine :: water : drought _____

6. carpenter : wood :: blacksmith : metal _____

7. fragrance : flower :: stench : garbage _____

8. soil : erode :: metal : corrode _____

9. white : vanilla :: brown : chocolate _____

10. insect : entomology :: reptile : herpetology _____

11. clippers : cut :: pliers : grip _____

12. critic : review :: journalist : reports _____

13. absorbent : cotton :: repellent : vinyl _____

14. sentry : guard :: courier : deliver _____

Completing Analogies

Choose the best pair of words to complete this analogy.

nitrogen **:** decomposition **: :** ____

    a.   plant   **:**   photosynthesize

    b.   cellulose   **:**   paper

    c.   oxygen   **:**   photosynthesis

    d.   oxidation   **:**   rust

1.   Each word pair should have the same type of relationship. State the relationship shown in the first word pair.

           Nitrogen is a product of the process of decomposition.

2.   Each word pair should show a similar relationship. Look at the choices given. Which pairs show a similar relationship?

           _____

Choices **a, c,** and **d** seem possible. All three include a process. In choice **b,** paper is a product of cellulose. However, cellulose is not a process; it is the part of the plant used to make paper. Also, the order of the words is switched to read *cellulose is a product of paper.* In choice **a,** *photosynthesize* is a process, but it is a verb not a noun. The pair has an object-action relationship that shows what a plant does rather than what it produces.

3.   The arrangement of each word pair should be the same. Look at choices **c** and **d.** Which pair has the same arrangement as the first pair? _____

In choice **d,** rust is a product of the process of oxidation, but the word order is different from the first pair. Therefore, the best choice is **c.** State the relationship shown in choice **c.**

           _____

Recognizing Correct Analogies

DIRECTIONS: An analogy compares two word pairs that have the same relationship. If the analogy is correct, classify the relationship using the categories listed. If the analogy is incorrect, classify the relationship shown in the first pair of words and rewrite the second pair of words to match. Categories: *antonym, association, synonym, kind of, object-action, part of, product of, something used to*

1. snake **is to** slither **AS** mouse **is to** rodent

   <u>Object-action: A snake slithers, a mouse scampers (or scurries).</u>

2. straight **is to** direct **AS** crooked **is to** uneven

   _____

3. furnace **is to** heat **AS** fan **is to** blow

   _____

4. tusk **is to** elephant **AS** deer **is to** antler

   _____

5. sonic **is to** sound **AS** optic **is to** vision

   _____

6. ascend **is to** descend **AS** fall **is to** rise

   _____

Complete the Analogy—Select

DIRECTIONS: Circle the best word to complete each analogy. State the relationship.

EXAMPLE

1. ballerina : dance : : acrobat : _____

   Relationship: <u>A ballerina is someone who dances,</u>

   <u>and an acrobat is someone who tumbles.</u>

   gymnast
   (tumble)
   circus
   somersault

2. deep : lake : : shallow : _____

   Relationship: _____

   _____

   water
   surface
   ocean
   puddle

3. wallet : money : : backpack : _____

   Relationship: _____

   _____

   satchel
   books
   hike
   zipper

4. bank : river : : wall : _____

   Relationship: _____

   _____

   canyon
   lake
   cascade
   plateau

5. feeler : antenna : : talon : _____

   Relationship: _____

   _____

   insect
   claw
   sharp
   bird

Complete the Analogy—Select

DIRECTIONS: Circle the best word to complete each analogy. (Hint: Some word choices could be used as a noun or a verb.)

1. cartilage : shark : : bone : _____

   rigid
   chicken
   arm
   skeleton

2. waterfall : cascade : : stream : _____

   water
   puddle
   ocean
   river

3. runner : jog : : bicyclist : _____

   pedal
   leg
   bicycle
   race

4. flu : virus : : infection : _____

   illness
   cut
   cold
   bacteria

5. latitude : longitude : : horizontal : _____

   globe
   vertical
   line
   direction

6. senator : legislature : : judge : _____

   client
   law
   criminal
   judiciary

7. mansion : wealth : : shack : _____

   poverty
   hut
   shame
   money

Complete the Analogy—Select

DIRECTIONS: Circle the best word to complete each analogy. (Hint: Some word choices could be used as a noun or a verb.)

1. bird : preen :: cat : _____

    fur
    groom
    hiss
    tiger

2. lung : breathe :: stomach : _____

    food
    organ
    eat
    digest

3. cockpit : plane :: bridge : _____

    river
    ship
    bicycle
    captain

4. perspiration : skin :: transpiration : _____

    leaf
    vehicle
    water
    bacteria

5. inch : foot :: yard : _____

    pound
    meter
    mile
    measure

6. portrait : painting :: bust : _____

    art
    broken
    sculpture
    bronze

7. ice : melt :: water : _____

    fluid
    hot
    freeze
    cold

Complete the Analogy—Select

DIRECTIONS: Circle the best word to complete each analogy. (Hint: Some word choices could be used as a noun or a verb.)

1. obstruct : clear :: clog : _____

   block
   help
   shut
   open

2. sweet : sour :: bland : _____

   food
   spicy
   mild
   taste

3. banana : bunch :: grape : _____

   round
   green
   cluster
   vine

4. geologist : rock :: botanist : _____

   leaf
   plant
   water
   bacteria

5. slam dunk : basketball :: slap shot : _____

   hockey
   ball
   football
   player

6. absorb : sponge :: repel : _____

   water
   towel
   umbrella
   ocean

7. tiny : average :: big : _____

   huge
   size
   large
   little

Complete the Analogy—Select

DIRECTIONS: Circle the best word to complete each analogy. (Hint: Some word choices could be used as a noun or a verb.)

1. mason : brick : : carpenter : _____

    plan
    hammer
    build
    wood

2. pink : red : : gray : _____

    white
    black
    color
    dark

3. farce : slapstick : : parody : _____

    humor
    play
    music
    satire

4. tundra : biome : : pond : _____

    lake
    water
    habitat
    clime

5. thorax : insect : : chest : _____

    trunk
    body
    human
    bug

6. kerosene : solvent : : oil : _____

    cream
    lubricant
    cooking
    engine

7. shade : window : : lid : _____

    cover
    eye
    drape
    man

Complete the Analogy Pair

DIRECTIONS: Circle the letter of the word pair that best completes each analogy.

1. initial : intermediate : :
   a. first : last
   b. final : last
   c. middle : end
   d. beginning : middle

2. balloon : rise : :
   a. air : inflate
   b. submarine : dive
   c. ball : throw
   d. rain : cloud

3. monk : monastery : :
   a. priest : rabbi
   b. church : parish
   c. nun : convent
   d. haven : retreat

4. rings : Saturn : :
   a. clouds : Venus
   b. planet : sun
   c. moon : orbit
   d. Mars : red

5. psychology : mind : :
   a. brain : think
   b. biology : science
   c. neurology : brain
   d. think : learn

6. angora : rabbit : :
   a. leaf : plant
   b. wool : weave
   c. web : spider
   d. mohair : goat

7. macaroni : pasta : :
   a. dough : bread
   b. noodle : spaghetti
   c. basil : thyme
   d. goulash : stew

Complete the Analogy Pair

DIRECTIONS: Circle the letter of the word pair that best completes each analogy.

1. rhinestone : diamond : :
   a. amethyst : gem
   b. small : large
   c. fake : real
   d. rock : stone

2. delicate : fragile : :
   a. web : rope
   b. weak : strong
   c. sturdy : strong
   d. spider : web

3. shingle : roof : :
   a. hall : building
   b. tile : floor
   c. wood : metal
   d. jamb : window

4. hook : crochet : :
   a. hook : eye
   b. knit : yarn
   c. thread : stitch
   d. needle : sew

5. rich : poor : :
   a. wealthy : needy
   b. rich : wealthy
   c. gold : jewels
   d. rags : riches

6. ship : fleet : :
   a. boat : dock
   b. sailor : crew
   c. yacht : liner
   d. rudder : boat

7. schedule : time : :
   a. graph : record
   b. budget : money
   c. clock : hour
   d. train : bus

Complete the Analogy Pair

DIRECTIONS: Circle the letter of the word pair that best completes each analogy.

1. cup : pint : :
   - a. gallon : liter
   - b. inch : meter
   - c. water : milk
   - d. ounce : pound

2. marble : limestone : :
   - a. igneous : rock
   - b. amethyst : quartz
   - c. gold : silver
   - d. concrete : plaster

3. artifact : museum : :
   - a. fossil : dinosaur
   - b. body : tomb
   - c. painting : gallery
   - d. history : art

4. bear : hibernate : :
   - a. goose : migrate
   - b. feather : float
   - c. mole : rodent
   - d. egg : hatch

5. amnesia : memory : :
   - a. brain : thought
   - b. paralysis : movement
   - c. recall : forget
   - d. analgesic : pain

6. merchant : sell : :
   - a. clerk : shop
   - b. store : order
   - c. customer : buy
   - d. supply : warehouse

7. governor : state : :
   - a. sailor : navy
   - b. mayor : city
   - c. senator : vote
   - d. judge : law

Complete the Analogy Pair

DIRECTIONS: Circle the letter of the word pair that best completes each analogy.

1. wicker : willow : :
   - a. cotton : cloth
   - b. rattan : palm
   - c. silk : satin
   - d. wheat : grain

2. circumference : circle : :
   - a. square : rectangle
   - b. radius : circle
   - c. angle : triangle
   - d. perimeter : square

3. simile : compare : :
   - a. syllable : word
   - b. metaphor : idiom
   - c. hyperbole : exaggerate
   - d. hyphen : separate

4. solar : sun : :
   - a. star : galaxy
   - b. moon : Jupiter
   - c. lunar : moon
   - d. radar : sub

5. spaniel : dog : :
   - a. tabby : cat
   - b. cougar : lion
   - c. canine : animal
   - d. dog : wolf

6. Styrofoam : insulate : :
   - a. medicine : vaccine
   - b. construct : lumber
   - c. quinine : bark
   - d. metal : conduct

7. steeple : church : :
   - a. bell : tower
   - b. turret : castle
   - c. pew : seat
   - d. chimney : roof

Complete the Analogy Pair

DIRECTIONS: Circle the letter of the word pair that best completes each analogy.

1. snare : animals : :
   - a. web : spider
   - b. seine : fish
   - c. cage : zoo
   - d. kennel : dog

2. hedgehog : land : :
   - a. mouse : rodent
   - b. urchin : ocean
   - c. cactus : spine
   - d. bee : hive

3. canal : irrigate : :
   - a. pipe : plumbing
   - b. lake : reservoir
   - c. culvert : drain
   - d. dam : water

4. solo : one : :
   - a. some : many
   - b. trio : three
   - c. four : five
   - d. quintet : quartet

5. plant : harvest : :
   - a. farmer : till
   - b. seed : grow
   - c. fall : autumn
   - d. sow : reap

6. strand : hair : :
   - a. blade : grass
   - b. seed : grow
   - c. wool : lamb
   - d. fiber : weave

7. pharaoh : Egypt : :
   - a. ruler : king
   - b. tsar : Russia
   - c. knight : England
   - d. Arabia : Bedouin

Complete the Analogy Pair

DIRECTIONS: Circle the letter of the word pair that best completes each analogy.

1. fish : aquarium : :
   a. cage : lion
   b. cage : zoo
   c. lizard : desert
   d. snake : terrarium

2. nugget : gold : :
   a. wheat : grain
   b. kernel : corn
   c. ore : mine
   d. iron : metal

3. fructose : fruit : :
   a. honey : sugar
   b. beet : sucrose
   c. wood : tree
   d. lactose : milk

4. soft : hard : :
   a. rock : bone
   b. cotton : rock
   c. cotton : fur
   d. sweet : sugary

5. sculptor : bronze : :
   a. poet : words
   b. lute : play
   c. singer : choir
   d. artist : painting

6. armor : knight : :
   a. mace : weapon
   b. lid : pan
   c. snail : shell
   d. carapace : turtle

7. fertilizer : plant : :
   a. pesticide : weed
   b. seed : flower
   c. vitamins : human
   d. food : nutrition

Writing Analogies

When writing analogies, remember these three things:

1. Both word pairs should have the same type of relationship.

    apiary : bees :: aviary : birds

    An apiary is used to house bees. An aviary is used to house birds.

2. The relationship should work in the same way for each pair.

    paper : tree :: papyrus : reed

    Paper is made from a tree. Papyrus is a kind of paper made from a reed.

3. The parts of speech used in each pair should be the same.

    fire : burn :: water : quench

    A fire burns, and water quenches. Each pair is a noun with a verb.

4. Words in each pair should be in the same order.

    teacher : principal :: clerk : manager

    A teacher is supervised by a principal. A clerk is supervised by a manager.

Choose the best words to complete each analogy. Be sure to put the words in the correct order.

1. minister : church :: _____ : _____

    (rabbi, cathedral, synagogue, congregation, bishop)

2. syllable : word :: _____ : _____

    (prefix, sentence, noun, paragraph, root)

3. stroller : child :: _____ : _____

    (crib, wheelchair, baby, invalid, walker)

Complete the Analogy—Select

DIRECTIONS: Choose the correct words to complete each analogy and write them on the lines.

1. trench : ditch : : _____ : _____

    narrow
    irrigate
    stream
    river

2. builder : blueprint : : _____ : _____

    pattern
    fabric
    seamstress
    decorator

3. prune : plum : : _____ : _____

    grape
    apricot
    raisin
    jam

4. integer : whole : : _____ : _____

    fraction
    part
    numeral
    digit

5. escalator : incline : : _____ : _____

    transport
    lift
    elevator
    vertical

6. banker : money : : _____ : _____

    stocks
    taxes
    broker
    merchant

Complete the Analogy—Select

DIRECTIONS: Choose the correct words to complete each analogy and write them on the lines.

1. rigid : steel : : _____ : _____

rubber
flexible
metal
copper

2. lard : hog : : _____ : _____

cow
dairy
butter
steer

3. reservoir : water : : _____ : _____

grain
coal
granary
quarry

4. skeleton : body : : _____ : _____

bone
framework
support
house

5. gale : wind : : _____ : _____

sleet
rain
drizzle
downpour

6. pioneer : explorer : : _____ : _____

architect
creative
designer
accountant

Complete the Analogy—Supply

DIRECTIONS: Choose the correct words to complete each analogy and write them on the lines.

1. whisper : scream : : _____ : _____

    soft
    voice
    speak
    loud

2. harmony : discord : : _____ : _____

    peace
    solitude
    anger
    war

3. meadow : pasture : : _____ : _____

    park
    woods
    plain
    forest

4. glaze : pottery : : _____ : _____

    veneer
    plastic
    furniture
    polish

5. velocity : speed : : _____ : _____

    frequency
    sound
    gravity
    weight

6. fawn : doe : : _____ : _____

    foal
    heifer
    horse
    mare

Complete the Analogy—Supply

DIRECTIONS: Choose the correct words to complete each analogy and write them on the lines.

1. concave : flat : : _____ : _____

    hill
    plateau
    steep
    crater

2. house : suburb : : _____ : _____

    city
    tenement
    ranch
    rural

3. greeting : letter : : _____ : _____

    book
    closing
    chapter
    foreword

4. engine : machine : : _____ : _____

    motor
    heart
    human
    generator

5. corral : cattle : : _____ : _____

    farm
    chicken
    kennel
    dog

6. realtor : buyer : : _____ : _____

    tenant
    seller
    landlord
    lease

Complete the Analogy—Supply

DIRECTIONS: Write the best words to complete each analogy.

1. hump : camel : : _____ : _____

2. linen : flax : : _____ : _____

3. kangaroo : Australia : : _____ : _____

4. plunge : dive : : _____ : _____

5. team : league : : _____ : _____

6. bleach : whiten : : _____ : _____

Complete the Analogy—Supply

DIRECTIONS: Write the best words to complete each analogy.

1. tailor : suit : : _____ : _____

2. fast : cheetah : : _____ : _____

3. scour : scrub : : _____ : _____

4. broom : sweep : : _____ : _____

5. cardigan : sweater : :_____ :_____

6. algebra : math : :_____ : _____

Make the Analogy

DIRECTIONS: Using words from the box, make one analogy of each type listed. Use each word only once.

faculty	mustard	professor	tart	office	pepper
pupil	acidic	teacher	clerk	school	learn
tangy	clove	book	class	instruct	condiment
student	cubicle	sour	opinion	spice	library

Kind of

1. _____ : _____ :: _____ : _____

Part of

2. _____ : _____ :: _____ : _____

Synonym

3. _____ : _____ :: _____ : _____

Someone Who

4. _____ : _____ :: _____ : _____

Make the Analogy

DIRECTIONS: Make 4 analogies using words in the box. Use each word only once.

shoe	glove	tall	coat	ounce	volume
clutch	quart	small	big	warm	foot
toe	finger	lift	button	pound	kick
hand	inch	raise	weight	short	dry
slicker	pint	boot	lace	gallon	mitten

1. _____ : _____ : : _____ : _____

2. _____ : _____ : : _____ : _____

3. _____ : _____ : : _____ : _____

4. _____ : _____ : : _____ : _____

Make the Analogy

DIRECTIONS: Make 5 analogies using words in the box. Use each word only once.

hot	freeze	chilly	water	humid	unfeeling
sand	Arctic	dry	cold	iris	melt
glacier	desert	tree	flower	warm	affectionate
maple	ice	dune	snow	boil	friendly
arid	orchard	wet	garden	aloof	tropic

1. _____ : _____ : : _____ : _____

2. _____ : _____ : : _____ : _____

3. _____ : _____ : : _____ : _____

4. _____ : _____ : : _____ : _____

5. _____ : _____ : : _____ : _____

Game Directions

General Setup: Make a set of 80–100 word cards (one word per card) and 2 sets of classification cards using the lists on the next page.

Classification Rummy (for 2 or more players)

Each player takes 8 word cards. The rest of the word cards are placed face down in a pile. The classification cards are placed face down in a second pile. The first player draws 1 card from the classification pile. Using the 8 word cards, the player tries to make a word pair that matches the relationship shown on the classification card. If the player has a matching pair, then the two cards and the classification card are laid down face up. If the player can't make a pair, then 1 word card is discarded and a new card is drawn from the word pile. If the player still can't make a matching word pair, then the classification card is placed at the bottom of the pile. The turn is over. The next player takes a new classification card from the pile and the game continues. The game is over when 1 player runs out of cards or all the classification cards are used. The winner is the player with the most correct word pairs. (Matching pairs for the suggested word list are listed in the answer key. Teacher-developed cards will need a separate answer key.)

OPTION: Let students trade for a card that they need.

Make An Analogy (for 2 or more players)

Use all 80 word cards. Each player starts with 8 word cards. The rest of the word cards are placed in a pile. The goal is to make as many analogies as possible. If a player cannot make an analogy, then a new card is drawn from the pile and 1 card is discarded face up. The turn ends if the player still cannot make an analogy. When a player has an analogy, the 4 cards are laid down and 4 new cards are drawn. To keep the game moving, players may draw a card from the new word card pile or the discard pile. The game ends when all the cards in the pile are gone or when a player has no more cards. The winner is the player with the most (correct) analogies. (Analogies are verified from a list of the analogies possible in the game.)

OPTION: Players must place word pairs on the table as they try to make analogies. A player may take another player's word pair if it can be used to complete an analogy.

OPTION: Players start with 8 word cards and 3 classification cards each. The goal is to be the first player to complete 3 analogies. Players draw and discard words from the word card pile on each turn. Increase the number of cards used with larger groups. A student can also play alone, trying to make as many matches as possible.

Suggested Word Lists for Card Games

Use 3 x 5 blank index cards. Make 2 sets of classification cards, 1 word per card. Make a set of 80 to 100 word cards, 1 word per card. Write the word across the top so the cards can be held like playing cards. Use a minimum of 80 word cards per game. Suggestions for words are listed below. Possible word pairs and analogies that can be made from these cards are listed in the answer key on page 56. You can make your own sets of word cards using reading vocabulary, spelling words, etc. Words with multiple meanings add more variety and challenge. Be sure that you include a sufficient number of possible analogies to keep the game moving.

Classification Cards: Antonyms, Association, Characteristic of, Kind of, Object-Action, Part of a group, Part of a whole, Product of, Sequence, Someone who, Something used to, Synonyms (Make 2 sets of cards)

Suggested Word Cards (80 words)

The following words can be used as a start for the games. Feel free to add more words. Just be sure to include enough analogies.

algae, amber, ancient, archaeologist, armor, author, bird, blueprint, botanist, building, cactus, cat, claw, composer, concerto, contractor, cougar, current, deer, desert, dig, drink, dull, dune, fin, fish, flock, flower, fly, fossil, fragrant, gladiator, glass, golfer, kelp, knight, leap, lizard, mammal, manuscript, Middle Ages, modern, mouse, music, novel, ocean, old, outdated, owl, pitcher, plant, pounce, predator, prey, putt, rapid, reptile, river, Roman Empire, rose, sand, school, shark, sharp, shell, slow, sluggish, spine, stream, swift, swim, talon, thorn, throw, tuna, turtle, water, wave, wing, write

Answer Key

Note: Other answers may be possible on pages 1–4. Accept any reasonable answer.

Finding Common Attributes (p. 1)

1. kinds of containers
2. things made of glass
3. things that are woven
4. things that are round
5. things that are rough
6. things that are white
7. kinds of gases
8. things that float
9. things that smell sweet
10. things used to attach
11. animal coverings
12. things with thorns
13. things that have branches
14. things that are microscopic
15. figures of speech

Finding the Exception (p. 2)

2. All natural fabrics except **vinyl** (manmade)
3. All related to clothing except **margin** (paper)
4. All reptiles except **shark** (fish)
5. All liquid measures except **pound** (dry)
6. Kinds of vines except **potato**
7. Birds that fly except **ostrich**
8. Two-dimensional figures except **sphere**
9. All meat-eaters except **deer** (herbivore)
10. Shades of red except **ochre** (yellow)
11. Parts of speech except **prefix** (word part)

12. Human limbs except **heart** (organ)
13. Kinds of text except **photo**
14. Car styles except **catamaran** (boat)
15. All citrus fruits except **pear**

Seeing Relationships (p. 3)

1. bird, **fly**
2. wing, **bird**
3. wing, **fly**
4. bird, **worm**
   A fish eats a fly; a bird eats a worm.

Making Word Pairs (p. 4)

1. arm/boy, ball/throw/, arm/throw
2. board/wood, board/fence, fence/wall, fence/wood
3. fish/school, boy/school, fish (or boy)/swim
4. flag/wave, ship/sea, wave/sea
5. quilt/blanket, lid/cover, quilt (or blanket)/cover

Lesson: Classifying Word Pairs (p. 5)

1. A lion is part of a pride (group of lions); a horse is part of a herd (group of horses).
2. A beetle is a kind of insect; a crab is a kind of crustacean.
3. Wool is a product of sheep; leather is a product of cattle.

Reading Analogies (p. 8)

1. Bristle is part of a brush; tooth is part of a comb.

2. Veterinarian is someone who works with animals; physician is someone who works with people.
3. Rabbit is a kind of herbivore; wolf is a kind of carnivore.
4. A crevice is a narrow opening; a crevasse is a wide opening.
5. *Inflate* and *expand* are synonyms; *deflate* and *shrink* are synonyms.

Lesson: Classifying Analogies (p. 9)

1. Antonyms: Uncle is a male relative, aunt is female; nephew is a male relative, niece is female.
2. Something used to: A pedestal is used to support a statue; a tripod is used to support a camera.

Classification Analogies— Select (p. 12)

1. a   9. a
2. b   10. c
3. a   11. b
4. a   12. a
5. c   13. b
6. b   14. b
7. c   15. c
8. c

Comparative Analogies— Select (p. 14)

1. a   9. b
2. b   10. a
3. c   11. b
4. a   12. c
5. b   13. b

6. a   14. a
7. c   15. a
8. a

Classifying Analogies (p. 15)

2. **c.** Music is produced by a piano. A photo is produced by a camera.

3. **a.** A skeleton is part of a body. A framework is part of a house. Both provide support.

4. **b.** Medium is bigger than small. Average is bigger than petite.

5. **d.** Fresh is the opposite of stale. Crisp is the opposite of wilted.

6. **c.** Cola comes from a nut. Chocolate comes from a bean.

7. **a.** A tributary is a branch of a river. A capillary is a branch of an artery.

Classifying Analogies (p. 16)

1. b   8. d
2. c   9. b
3. b   10. a
4. d   11. d
5. a   12. c
6. d   13. b
7. a   14. a

Classifying Analogies (p. 17)

1. c   8. b
2. d   9. c
3. b   10. d
4. d   11. a
5. c   12. b
6. a   13. a
7. a   14. d

Descriptive Analogies—Select (p. 20)

1. c   9. a

2. b   10. c
3. a   11. a
4. c   12. b
5. b   13. c
6. b   14. a
7. a   15. c
8. b

Descriptive Analogies—Select (p. 21)

1. c   9. c
2. c   10. a
3. b   11. b
4. a   12. b
5. a   13. c
6. b   14. b
7. c   15. a
8. a

Classifying Analogies (p. 22)

1. **b.** In a food chain, grass is a kind of producer, and a rabbit is a kind of consumer.

2. **c.** A president is a leader associated with a democracy, and a king is a leader associated with a monarchy.

3. **b.** Taffeta is a kind of fabric, and taffy is a kind of candy.

4. **d.** Counterfeit and imitation are synonyms. Genuine and real are synonyms.

5. **a.** A bridge is used to cross a river; an overpass is used to cross a freeway.

6. **d.** Mild, gentle, soft, and tender are all synonyms.

7. **b.** Oil is a kind of liquid; nitrogen is a kind of gas.

Classifying Analogies (p. 23)

1. **b.** The Stone Age came

before the Bronze Age; the Dark Ages came before the Renaissance.

2. **a.** A balloon can float; a bird can fly.

3. **d.** The ribs support the open umbrella; the spokes support the wheel.

4. **c.** Milk is usually white in color; water is usually clear.

5. **d.** An octopus uses a tentacle to hold; a plant uses a tendril to hold.

6. **a.** A lung inflates with air when the diaphragm contracts.

7. **c.** A nose is made of cartilage; a jaw is made of bone.

Classifying Analogies (p. 24)

1. a   8. b
2. d   9. c
3. b   10. a
4. d   11. b
5. c   12. a
6. a   13. c
7. d   14. c

Classifying Analogies (p. 25)

1. **d.** (Sawdust is produced when wood is cut; chaff is produced when wheat is threshed.)

2. b

3. a

4. d

5. **b.** (d is not correct. Products would be milk and eggs.)

6. **c.** (Both are used to dispense measured amounts.)

7. **c.** (Decibel and fathom are types of measurement.)

8. a
9. **c.** (An axis supports a wheel; a fulcrum supports a lever. Both are pivot points.)
10. **b.** (Both are parts that overhang.)
11. **c.** (A lighthouse guides ships; a buoy marks dangers.)
12. **b.** (Both are parts left over. Residue is leftover paint; remnant is leftover fabric.)
13. a
14. **d.** (Mustard is made from a seed; ketchup is made from a tomato.)

Classifying Analogies (p.26)

1. **c.** (The Roman goddess of love and god of war.)
2. a
3. d
4. b
5. **c.** (The lack of food and water.)
6. a
7. d
8. b
9. d
10. **c.** (Entomology is the study of insects; herpetology is the study of reptiles.)
11. b
12. a
13. d
14. a

Lesson: Completing Analogies (p. 27)

2. **a, c, d**
3. **c.** Oxygen is a product of photosynthesis.

Recognizing Correct Analogies (p. 28)

2. Synonym
3. Something used to: fan is to cool
4. Part of: antler is to deer
5. Association
6. Antonym: rise is to fall

Complete the Analogy—Select (p. 29)

2. **puddle.** A lake is a deep body of water; a puddle is a shallow body of water.
3. **books.** A wallet is used to carry money; a backpack is used to carry books.
4. **canyon.** A bank is the side part of a river; a wall is the side part of a canyon.
5. **claw.** A feeler is an antenna; a talon is a claw.

Complete the Analogy—Select (p. 30)

1. chicken (part of)
2. river (synonym)
3. pedal (object-action)
4. bacteria (product of)
5. vertical (antonym)
6. judiciary (someone who)
7. poverty (association)

Complete the Analogy—Select (p. 31)

1. groom (object-action)
2. digest (used to)
3. ship (part of)
4. leaf (association)
5. mile (sequence)
6. sculpture (kind of)
7. freeze (object-action)

Complete the Analogy—Select (p. 32)

1. open (antonym)
2. spicy (antonym)
3. cluster (part of)
4. plant (someone who)
5. hockey (association)
6. umbrella (characteristic)
7. huge (sequence)

Complete the Analogy—Select (p. 33)

1. wood (someone who)
2. black (sequence)
3. satire (synonym)
4. habitat (kind of)
5. human (part of)
6. lubricant (kind of)
7. eye (part of)

Complete the Analogy Pair (p. 34)

1. d (sequence)
2. b (object-action)
3. c (part of)
4. a (association)
5. c (association)
6. d (product of)
7. d (kind of)

Complete the Analogy Pair (p. 35)

1. c (kind of gem)
2. c (synonym)
3. b (part of)
4. d (used to)
5. a (antonym)
6. b (part of group)
7. b (used to organize)

Complete the Analogy Pair (p. 36)

1. d (sequence)
2. b (kind of)
3. c (part of)
4. a (object-action)
5. b (association—loss of)
6. c (someone who)

7. b (association)

**Complete the Analogy Pair
(p. 37)**

1. b (product of)
2. d (part of—boundary)
3. c (used to—figures of speech)
4. c (association)
5. a (kind of)
6. d (used to)
7. b (part of—both towers)

**Complete the Analogy Pair
(p. 38)**

1. b (used to)
2. b (association)
3. c (used to)
4. b (synonym)
5. d (sequence)
6. a (part of)
7. b (association)

**Complete the Analogy Pair
(p. 39)**

1. d (part of)
2. b (association)
3. d (product of)
4. b (characteristic)
5. a (someone who)
6. d (used to)
7. c (used to)

**Lesson: Writing Analogies
(p. 40)**

1. rabbi, synagogue
2. noun, sentence (or sentence, paragraph)
3. wheelchair, invalid

**Complete the Analogy—
Select (p. 41)**

1. **stream, river** (Synonyms)
2. **seamstress, pattern** A builder follows a blueprint; a seamstress follows a pattern.
3. **raisin, grape** A prune is a dried plum; a raisin is a dried grape.
4. **fraction, part** An integer is a whole number; a fraction is part of a number.
5. **elevator, vertical** An escalator is at an incline; an elevator lift is vertical.
6. **broker, stocks** A banker works with money; a broker with stocks.

**Complete the Analogy—
Select (p. 42)**

1. **flexible, rubber** Steel is rigid; rubber is flexible.
2. **butter, cow** Lard comes from a hog; butter comes from a cow.
3. **granary, grain** A reservoir is used to store water; a granary is used to store grain.
4. **framework, house** A skeleton supports the body; a framework supports the house.
5. **downpour, rain** A gale is a very strong wind; a downpour is a very strong rain.
6. **architect, designer** A pioneer is a kind of explorer; an architect is a kind of designer.

**Complete the Analogy—
Supply (p. 43)**

1. **soft, loud** A whisper is soft; a scream is loud.
2. **peace, war** Antonyms
3. **woods, forest** Synonyms
4. **veneer, furniture** A glaze is a thin coating on the outside of pottery; veneer is a thin layer on the outside of furniture.
5. **frequency, sound** Velocity is a measurement of speed; frequency is a measurement of sound.
6. **foal, mare** A fawn comes from a doe; a foal comes from a mare.

**Complete the Analogy—
Supply (p. 44)**

1. **crater, plateau** A crater is concave in shape; a plateau is flat.
2. **tenement, city** A house is associated with a suburb; a tenement is associated with a city.
3. **foreword, book** A greeting is the opening of a letter; a foreword is the beginning of a book.
4. **heart, human** An engine powers a machine; the heart powers the human body.
5. **kennel, dog** A corral is used to hold cattle; a kennel is used to hold a dog.
6. **landlord, tenant** A realtor works with a buyer; a landlord works with a tenant.

**Complete the Analogy—
Supply (p. 45)**

The following answers are possible. Accept any reasonable answer that fits the criteria given on page 40.

1. pouch/kangaroo; shell/turtle (part of)
2. leather/cow, silk/worm,

honey/bee (product of)

3. panda/China; elephant/
India (association)

4. leap/jump; fall/tumble
(synonyms)

5. class/school; school/
district (part of group)

6. dye/color; soap/clean
(something used to)

Complete the Analogy—Supply (p. 46)

1. seamstress/clothes;
milliner/hats (someone
who)

2. slow/turtle; large/elephant
(characteristic)

3. polish/shine; mop/wipe
(synonyms)

4. sponge/wipe; cloth/dust
(something used to)

5. blazer/jacket; parka/coat
(kind of)

6. biology/science (kind of)

Make the Analogy (p. 47)

1. Kind of
clove/spice AS pepper
(mustard)/condiment

2. Part of
cubicle/office AS library/
school
professor (or teacher)/
faculty AS student (pupil)/
class

3. Synonym
teacher/professor AS
student/pupil
sour/acidic AS tart/tangy

4. Someone Who
professor (teacher)/instruct
AS student (pupil)/learn
professor(teacher)/school
AS clerk/office

Make the Analogy (p. 48)

Antonyms
tall/short AS big /small

Object-Action
hand/lift (clutch) AS foot/
kick

Part of
toe/foot AS finger/hand
toe/boot (shoe) AS finger/
glove (mitten)
button/coat (slicker) AS
lace/shoe (boot)

Sequence
pint/quart AS ounce/pound
OR inch/foot

Something used to
shoe/glove OR boot/mitten
AS foot/hand
glove (mitten)/hand AS
(boot) shoe/foot
ounce (pound)/weight AS
pint (gallon)/volume
coat/warm AS slicker/dry

Synonyms
tall/big AS short/small OR
lift/raise
glove/mitten AS boot/shoe

Make the Analogy (p. 49)

Antonyms
hot (warm)/cold (chilly)
AS dry/wet
cold/affectionate AS
warm/unfeeling

Synonyms
warm/hot AS cold/chilly
friendly (warm)/
affectionate AS cold/
unfeeling
arid/dry AS wet/humid

Characteristic
dry (arid)/desert AS cold/
Arctic
sand/desert AS ice/Arctic

ice/glacier AS sand/dune
melt/ice (snow) AS freeze/
water OR boil/water
hot/tropic AS cold/Arctic

Part of
sand/desert AS snow/
Arctic OR glacier/Arctic
AS dune/desert
tree (maple)/orchard AS
flower (iris)/garden

Kind of
iris/flower AS maple/tree

CARD GAMES

Possible answers using the
suggested word cards.

CLASSIFICATION RUMMY

Antonyms
sharp/dull
modern/old (ancient)
current/outdated
rapid/slow
sluggish/swift

Association
cactus (dune)/desert
kelp (wave)/ocean
gladiator/Roman Empire
knight/Middle Ages

Characteristic of
sharp/claw(talon)
sharp/thorn (spine)
fragrant/rose (flower)
old (ancient)/fossil
water/wave
sand/dune

Kind of
cougar/cat
tuna (shark)/fish
owl/bird
lizard/reptile
cougar (owl, shark)/
predator
mouse (tuna, deer)/prey

rose/flower

cactus/plant

concerto/music

Object-Action

fish (tuna)/swim

bird (owl)/fly

golfer/putt

pitcher/throw

cougar (cat)/pounce

deer/leap

Part of

spine/cactus

thorn/rose

talon/owl

claw/cougar

fin/fish (tuna)

wing/bird (owl)

current/ocean

rapid/river

sand/desert

water/ocean

fish (tuna)/school

bird/flock

Product of

amber/fossil

glass/sand

novel/author

concerto/composer

Sequence

mouse/owl (size)

deer/cougar (size)

blueprint/building

manuscript/novel

Someone Who

contractor/building (blueprint)

author/write (novel, maunscript)

archaeologist/fossil (dig)

botanist/plant

composer/concerto (music)

Something Used to

shovel/dig

glass/drink

wing/fly

fin/swim

armor/knight

shell/turtle

Synonyms

talon/claw

thorn/spine

current/modern

old/outdated (ancient)

rapid/swift

slow/sluggish

MAKE AN ANALOGY

ANTONYM

sharp/dull AS current/outdated AS modern/ old(ancient)

rapid/slow AS swift/sluggish

ASSOCIATION

kelp/ocean AS cactus/desert

gladiator/Roman Empire AS knight/Middle Ages

CHARACTERISTIC

sharp/talon (claw) AS old (ancient)/fossil

sharp/thorn (spine) AS fragrant/ rose (flower)

water/wave AS sand/dune

KIND OF

cougar/cat AS tuna (shark)/fish OR owl/bird OR lizard/reptile

owl/predator AS mouse/prey

cougar/predator AS deer/prey

shark/predator AS tuna/prey

rose/flower AS cactus/plant

OBJECT-ACTION

golfer/putt AS pitcher/throw

bird (owl)/fly AS fish (tuna)/ swim

cougar/pounce AS deer/leap

PART OF

spine/cactus AS thorn/rose

talon/owl AS claw/cougar

fin/fish (tuna, shark) AS wing/

bird (owl)

fish (tuna)/school AS bird/flock

wave/ocean AS dune/desert

sand/desert AS water/ocean (river, stream)

current/ocean AS rapid/river

PRODUCT OF

amber/fossil AS glass/sand

novel (manuscript)/author AS concerto (music)/composer

Sequence

mouse/owl AS deer/cougar (size)

blueprint/building AS manuscript/novel

SOMEONE WHO

archaeologist/fossil AS botanist/plant AS contractor/ building

archaeologist/dig AS author /write

author/manuscript AS contractor/blueprint

author/novel AS composer/ concerto (music)

SOMETHING USED TO

armor/knight AS shell/turtle

wing/fly AS fin/swim

shovel/dig AS glass/drink

SYNONYMS

talon/claw AS thorn/spine OR river/stream

current/modern AS old/ outdated(ancient)

rapid/swift AS slow/sluggish

READING DETECTIVE® B1 SAMPLE ACTIVITY

On the following pages is a sample activity from our popular reading series, *Reading Detective®*. There are currently three books in the series, *Reading Detective® Beginning,* grades 3–4, *Reading Detective® A1,* grades 5–6, and *Reading Detective® B1,* grades 7–8. The following sample is from the *B1* book.

- The *Reading Detective®* series is based on national and state reading standards. These books, however, go beyond current reading comprehension materials by requiring 1) a higher level of analysis and 2) evidence to support answers. Students are asked to read a passage, then answer a variety of questions, supporting their answers with specific evidence from the passage. This skill, required by most state standards, is seldom addressed in the available reading materials.

- Skills covered include basic reading skills such as reading for detail and identifying the main idea, literary analysis skills such as analyzing character traits and identifying setting, and critical thinking skills such as making inferences and distinguishing between cause and effect.

- Each book includes excerpts from works of award-winning authors and original fiction in a variety of genres: mystery, fantasy, adventure, humor. Nonfiction articles cover topics that coincide with classroom curricula in science, social studies, math, and the arts.

- For further samples and information on the *Reading Detective®* series, see our Web site at www. criticalthinking.com.